MUSEUM

MUSEUM

poems by

RITA DOVE

CARNEGIE MELLON UNIVERSITY PRESS
PITTSBURGH 1992

ACKNOWLEDGMENTS:

Some of these poems have appeared in the following magazines:

The Georgia Review: "The Hill Has Something to Say," "Receiving the Stigmata;" *Kenyon Review*: "Grape Sherbet;" *Massachusetts Review*: "Anti-Father," "Three Days of Forest, a River, Free;" *The Nation*: "The Ants of Argos;" *National Forum*: "The Fish in the Stone;" *New Orleans Review*: "The Left-Handed Cellist;" *Ontario Review*: "Eastern European Eclogues," "Parsley;" *Poetry*: "Agosta the Winged Man and Rasha the Black Dove," "Dusting," "November for Beginners" (© 1981 Modern Poetry Association); "Flirtation" (© 1982 Modern Poetry Association); *Poetry NOW*: "Lines Muttered in Sleep," "Tou Wan Speaks to her Husband, Liu Sheng;" *The Reaper*: "At the German Writers Conference in Munich," "Primer for the Nuclear Age," "Shakespeare Say;" *Tesseract*: "Catherine of Alexandria," "Catherine of Siena," "Reading Hölderlin on the Patio with the Aid of a Dictionary."

Reprint of the 1929 painting "Agosta, der Flügelmensch und Rasha, die schwarze Taube" on the cover of this book by permission of the artist, Christian Schad (1894-1982). The original is painted in color, oil on canvas, 120 x 80 cm. The author wishes to thank Bettina Schad for her kind cooperation.
The quote at the beginning of section II ("In the Bulrush") is from the song "Sun is shining" by Bob Marley. © 1977 Bob Marley Music Ltd. Used by permission.

Library of Congress Catalog Card Number 82-71663
ISBN 0-88748-147-7
Printed and bound in the United States of America
First Classic Contemporary printing, April 1992

10 9 8 7 6 5 4 3

for nobody
who made us possible

TABLE OF CONTENTS

III. MY FATHER'S TELESCOPE

IV. PRIMER FOR THE NUCLEAR AGE

Notes

DUSTING

Every day a wilderness— no
shade in sight. Beulah
patient among knickknacks,
the solarium a rage
of light, a grainstorm
as her gray cloth brings
dark wood to life.

Under her hand scrolls
and crests gleam
darker still. What
was his name, that
silly boy at the fair with
the rifle booth? And his kiss and
the clear bowl with one bright
fish, rippling
wound!

Not Michael—
something finer. Each dust
stroke a deep breath and
the canary in bloom.
Wavery memory: home
from a dance, the front door
blown open and the parlor
in snow, she rushed
the bowl to the stove, watched
as the locket of ice

dissolved and he
swam free.

That was years before
Father gave her up
with her name, years before
her name grew to mean
Promise, then
Desert-in-Peace.
Long before the shadow and
sun's accomplice, the tree.

Maurice.

I
THE HILL HAS SOMETHING TO SAY

Here lies
Ike Tell:
Heathen.
No chance of Heaven,
No fear of Hell.

—tombstone near
Weimar, Texas

THE FISH IN THE STONE

The fish in the stone
would like to fall
back into the sea.

He is weary
of analysis, the small
predictable truths.
He is weary of waiting
in the open,
his profile stamped
by a white light.

In the ocean the silence
moves and moves

and so much is unnecessary!
Patient, he drifts
until the moment comes
to cast his
skeletal blossom.

The fish in the stone
knows to fail is
to do the living
a favor.

He knows why the ant
engineers a gangster's
funeral, garish
and perfectly amber.
He knows why the scientist
in secret delight
strokes the fern's
voluptuous braille.

THE ANTS OF ARGOS

There stood the citadel— nothing left.
We climbed it anyway, if for no other reason
than to say we'd been someplace
where earth and air had been quietly
rearranged. Nothing was left

but you and me, standing above the small
and empty harbor flashing blue.
Around us wild thyme ached in mauve
and sun-baked stones fumed piquant
wherever shepherd boys had pissed

to hear them sizzle. Even the ants,
marching skyward, had been in Corinth.

PITHOS

Climb
into a jar
and live
for a while.

Chill earth.
No stars
in this stone
sky.

You have ceased
to ache.

Your spine is
a flower.

NESTOR'S BATHTUB

As usual, legend got it all
wrong: Nestor's wife was the one
to crouch under
jug upon jug of fragrant water poured
until the small room steamed.
But where was Nestor—
on his throne before the hearth,
counting the jars of oil
in storeroom 34, or
at the Trojan wars
while his wife with her white hands
scraped the dirt from a lover's back
with a bronze scalpel?

Legend, as usual, doesn't
say. But this heap of limestone
blocks— look how they fell, blasted
by the force of olive oil
exploding in the pot, look
at the pattern left in stucco
from the wooden columns, sixty
flutings, look at the shards
scattered in the hall where
jars spilled from the second floor,
oil spreading in flames
to the lady's throne.

For the sake of legend only the tub
stands, tiny and voluptuous
as a gravy dish.
And the blackened remains of ivory

combs and 2,853 tall-stemmed
drinking cups in the pantry—
these, too, survived
when the clay pots screamed
and stones sprang their sockets
and the olive trees grew into the hill.

THE HILL HAS SOMETHING TO SAY

but isn't talking.
Instead the valley groans as the wind,
amphoric,
hoots its one bad note.
Halfway up, we stop to peek
through smudged pine: this is Europe
and its green terraces.

*

and takes its time.
What's left
to climb's inside us,
earth rising, stupified.

*

: it's not all in the books
(but maps don't lie).
The hill has a right
to stand here, one knob
in the coiled spine of a peasant
who, forgetting to flee, simply
lay down forever.

*

bootstrap and spur
harrow and pitchfork
a bugle a sandal
clay head of a pipe

*

(For all we know
the wind's inside us, pacing
our lungs. For all we know
it's spring and the ground
moistens as raped maids break
to blossom. What's invisible
sings, and we bear witness.)

*

if we would listen! Underfoot
slow weight, Scavenger Time,
and the little old woman
who lives there still.

THE COPPER BEECH

Aristocrat among patriarchs, this
noble mutation is the best
specimen of Rococo

in the park of the castle
at Erpenberg.
The widely-traveled Baroness

returned
from a South American expedition
with any number of plants and a few

horticultural innovations.
This trailing beech became Erpenberg's
tree of grief, their

melancholy individualist,
the park philosopher.
Eight meters above lawn

the tousled crown
rises, her many plaited branches falling
like green water

earthwards, a cascade of leaves.
The aesthetic principles
of the period: branches

pruned late to heal
into knots, proud flesh ascending
the trunk:

living architecture.

TOU WAN SPEAKS TO HER HUSBAND, LIU SHENG

I will build you a house
of limited chambers
but it shall last
forever: four rooms
hewn in the side of stone
for you, my
only conqueror.

In the south room all
you will need for the journey
—a chariot, a
dozen horses—
opposite,

a figurine household
poised in servitude
and two bronze jugs, worth more
than a family pays in taxes
for the privilege to stay
alive, a year, together. . .

but you're bored.
Straight ahead then, the hall
leading to you, my
constant
emperor. Here
when the stench of your
own diminishing
drives you to air (but

you will find none), here
an incense burner
in the form of the mountain
around you, where hunters pursue
the sacred animal

and the peaks are drenched
in sun.

        For those times
in your niche when darkness
oppresses, I will set you
a lamp. (And a statue
of the palace girl you most
frequently coveted.)

And for your body,
two thousand jade wafers
with gold thread puzzled
to a brilliant envelope,
a suit to keep
the shape of your death—

when you are long light and clouds
over the earth, just as the legends prophesy.

CATHERINE OF ALEXANDRIA

Deprived of learning and
   the chance to travel,
no wonder sainthood
   came as a voice

in your bed—
   and what went on
each night was fit
   for nobody's ears

but Jesus'. His
   breath of a lily.
His spiraling
   pain. Each morning

the nightshirt bunched
   above your waist—
a kept promise,
   a ring of milk.

CATHERINE OF SIENA

You walked the length of Italy
to find someone to talk to.
You struck the boulder at the roadside
since fate has doors everywhere.
Under the star-washed dome
of heaven, warm and dark

as the woolens stacked on cedar
shelves back home in your
father's shop, you prayed
until tears streaked the sky.
No one stumbled across your path.
No one unpried your fists as you slept.

RECEIVING THE STIGMATA

There is a way to enter a field
empty-handed, your shoulder
behind you and air tightening.

The kite comes by itself,
a spirit on a fluttering string.

Back when people died for
the smallest reasons, there was
always a field to walk into.
Simple men fell to their knees
below the radiant crucifix
and held out their palms

in relief. Go into the field
and it will reward. Grace

is a string growing straight
from the hand. Is
the hatchet's shadow on the
rippling green.

BOCCACCIO: THE PLAGUE YEARS

Even at night the air rang and rang.
Through the thick swirled glass
he watched the priests sweep past
in their peaked hoods, collecting death.
On each stoop a dish burning sweet
clotted smoke. He closed his eyes
to hear the slap
of flesh onto flesh, a
liquid crack like a grape
as it breaks on the tongue.

As a boy he had slipped
along the same streets, in love with
he didn't know whom. O the
reeded sonatinas and torch
flick on the chill slick sides
of the bridge and steam
rising in plumes
from the slaughterhouse vents—
twenty years.

Rolling out of the light
he leaned his cheek
against the rows of bound leather:
cool water. Fiammetta!
He had described her
a hundred ways; each time
she had proven unfaithful. If only
he could crack this city in two
so the moon would scour
the wormed streets clean! Or
walk away from it all, simply
falling in love again. . . .

FIAMMETTA BREAKS HER PEACE

I've watched them, mother, and I know
the signs. The first day, rigor.
Staggering like drunks, they
ram the room's sharp edges
with the most delicate bodily parts
and feel no pain. Unable
to sleep, they shiver beneath
all the quilts in the house,
panic gnawing a silver path to the brain.

Day two is fever, the bright
stream clogged, eyes rodent
red. No one weeps anymore; just
waits, for appear they must—
in the armpits, at the groin—
hard, blackened apples.
Then, at least, there is certainty,
an odd kind of relief;
a cross comes on the door.

A few worthy citizens gather possessions
around them and spend time
with fine foods, wine and music
behind closed drapes. Having left
the world already, they are surprised
when the world finds them again.
Still others carouse from tavern
to tavern, doing exactly as they please. . . .

And to think he wanted me
beautiful! To be his fresh air

and my breasts two soft
spiced promises. *Stand still,* he said
once, *and let me admire you.*

All is infection, mother— and avarice,
and self-pity, and fear!
We shall sit quietly in this room,
and I think we'll be spared.

II
IN THE BULRUSH

When the morning
gather the rainbow,
want you to know
I'm a rainbow, too.

—*Bob Marley*

NOVEMBER FOR BEGINNERS

Snow would be the easy
way out— that softening
sky like a sigh of relief
at finally being allowed
to yield. No dice.
We stack twigs for burning
in glistening patches
but the rain won't give.

So we wait, breeding
mood, making music
of decline. We sit down
in the smell of the past
and rise in a light
that is already leaving.
We ache in secret,
memorizing

a gloomy line
or two of German.
When spring comes
we promise to act
the fool. Pour,
rain! Sail, wind,
with your cargo of zithers!

READING HÖLDERLIN ON THE PATIO
WITH THE AID OF A DICTIONARY

One by one, the words
give themselves
up, white flags dispatched
from a silent camp.

When had my shyness returned?

This evening, the sky refused
to lie down. The sun crouched
behind leaves, but the trees
had long since walked away.
The meaning that surfaces

comes to me aslant and
I go to meet it, stepping
out of my body
word for word, until I am

everything at once: the perfume
of the world in which
I go under,
a skindiver
remembering air.

SHAKESPEARE SAY

He drums the piano wood,
crowing.

Champion Jack in love
and in debt,
in a tan walking suit
with a flag on the pocket,
with a red eye
for women, with a
diamond-studded
ear, with sand
in a mouthful of mush—

poor me
poor me
I keep on drifting
like a ship out
on the sea

That afternoon two students
from the Akademie
showed him the town.
Munich was misbehaving,
whipping
his ass to ice
while his shoes
soaked through. His guides
pointed at a clock
in a blue-tiled house.
And tonight

every song he sings
is written by Shakespeare
and his mother-in-law.
I love you, baby,
but it don't mean
a goddam thing.
In trouble

with every woman he's
ever known, all of them
ugly— skinny legs, lie gap
waiting behind the lips
to suck him in.

Going down slow
crooning *Shakespeare say*
man must be
careful what he kiss
when he drunk,
going down
for the third set
past the stragglers
at the bar,
the bourbon in his hand
some bitch's cold
wet heart,
the whole joint

stinking on beer;
in love and winning
now, so even the mistakes
sound like jazz,
poor me, moaning
so no one hears:

my home's in Louisiana,
my voice is wrong,
I'm broke and can't hold
my piss;
my mother told me
there'd be days like this.

THREE DAYS OF FOREST, A RIVER, FREE

The dogs have nothing better
to do than bark; duty's whistle
slings a bright cord
around their throats.
I'll stand here all night
if need be, no more real
than a tree when no moon shines.

The terror of waking is a trust
drawn out unbearably
until nothing, not even love,
makes it easier, and yet
I love this life:

three days of forest,
the mute riot of leaves.

Who can point out a smell
but a dog? The way is free
to the river. Tell me,
Lord, how it feels
to burst out like a rose.

Blood rises in my head—
I'm there.
Faint tongue, dry fear,
I think I lost you to the dogs,
so far off now they're no
more than a chain of bells
ringing darkly, underground.

BANNEKER

What did he do except lie
under a pear tree, wrapped in
a great cloak, and meditate
on the heavenly bodies?
Venerable, the good people of Baltimore
whispered, shocked and more than
a little afraid. After all it was said
he took to strong drink.
Why else would he stay out
under the stars all night
and why hadn't he married?

But who would want him! Neither
Ethiopian nor English, neither
lucky nor crazy, a capacious bird
humming as he penned in his mind
another enflamed letter
to President Jefferson— he imagined
the reply, polite and rhetorical.
Those who had been to Philadelphia
reported the statue
of Benjamin Franklin
before the library

his very size and likeness.
A wife? No, thank you.
At dawn he milked
the cows, then went inside
and put on a pot to stew
while he slept. The clock
he whittled as a boy
still ran. Neighbors
woke him up
with warm bread and quilts.
At nightfall he took out

his rifle— a white-maned
figure stalking the darkened
breast of the Union— and
shot at the stars, and by chance
one went out. Had he killed?
I assure thee, my dear Sir!
Lowering his eyes to fields
sweet with the rot of spring, he could see
a government's domed city
rising from the morass and spreading
in a spiral of lights. . . .

IN THE BULRUSH

Cut a cane that once
grew in the river.
Lean on it. Weigh

a stone in your hands
and put it down again.
Watch it moss over.

Strike the stone
to see if it's thinking
of water.

DELFT

Flat, with variations. Not
the table but the cloth.
As if a continent
raging westward, staggered
at the sight of
so much water, sky
on curdling sky.

Wherever I walk
the earth's soft
mouth suckles.
These clumps of beeches,
glazed trunks
green with age.
Each brick house the original
oven, fired to stay
incipient mold,

while in the hour
of least resolve
the starched sheets
scratch the insomniac wife
to bravado. *At least,*
she whispers,

we dine in style.
And our sceneries
please. We may be standing
on a porch
open to the world
but the house behind us
is sinking.

IKE

Grew hair for fun.
Found a mouth harp.
Scared away the bees.

The creek and the ford
Build step by step.
Sassy finch: kept time
To his creaking knee.

Up the hill fine
Families benched
And wailing. Organ
Panting, a diseased
Lung.

Marched outback.
Shot a cottonmouth.

Heard it twitch
The whole night long.

AGOSTA THE WINGED MAN
AND RASHA THE BLACK DOVE

Schad paced the length of his studio
and stopped at the wall,
                              staring
at a blank space. Behind him
the clang and hum of Hardenbergstrasse, its
automobiles and organ grinders.
                              Quarter to five.
His eyes traveled
to the plaster scrollwork
on the ceiling. Did *that*
                              hold back heaven?
He could not leave his skin— once
he'd painted himself in a new one,
silk green, worn
like a shirt.
                    He thought
of Rasha, so far from Madagascar,
turning slowly in place as
the boa constrictor
coiled counterwise its
                              heavy love. How
the spectators gawked, exhaling
beer and sour herring sighs.
When the tent lights dimmed,
Rasha went back to her trailer and plucked
a chicken for dinner.
                         The canvas,

not his eye, was merciless.
He remembered Katja the Russian
aristocrat, late
for every sitting,
                    still fleeing
the October Revolution—
how she clutched her sides
and said not
                    one word. Whereas Agosta

(the doorbell rang)
was always on time, lip curled
as he spoke in wonder of women
                              trailing
backstage to offer him
the consummate bloom of their lust.

Schad would place him
on a throne, a white sheet tucked
over his loins, the black suit jacket
thrown off like a cloak.
Agosta had told him
                    of the medical students
at the Charité,
that chill arena
                where he perched on
a cot, his torso
exposed, its crests and fins
a colony of birds, trying
to get out . . .
                and the students,
lumps caught
in their throats, taking notes.

Ah, Rasha's
              foot on the stair.
She moved slowly, as if she carried
the snake around her body
always.
                    Once
she brought fresh eggs into
the studio, flecked and
warm as breath.
                    Agosta in
classical drapery, then,
and Rasha at his feet.
Without passion. Not
the canvas
              but their gaze,
              so calm,
was merciless.

AT THE GERMAN WRITERS
CONFERENCE IN MUNICH

In the large hall of the Hofbräuhaus
above the heads of the members
of the board, taut and white
as skin (not mine),
tacked across a tapestry
this banner:

Association of German
Writers in the Union of Printers
and Paper Manufacturers.

Below it some flowers,
typical medieval,
and a maiden's feet
under a printed silk gown.
The tapestry pokes out

all over: a woman
in a green kerchief,
a king with a scepter and
crown puffed like a soufflé;
an ash-blonde princess
by birthright permitted
to bare her crinklets
to sun and smoke. Then another
lady-in-waiting, this time
in a white kerchief
and a white horse craning
to observe the royal party.

At the bottom strip of needlework
four flat bread loaves.
Far in the eaves
two doves signify
a union endorsed

by God and the Church.
Further, green hills
rolling with pine.

Above them all a banner
unfurled and inscribed
in Latin. Maybe it says
Association of Tapestrers
in the Union of Wives
and Jewish Dyers.
No one's feet are visible
but those dainty shoes
beneath the printed silk
that first caught my eye,
and the grotesquely bent
fetlock-to-ivory hoof
of the horse. And both
are in flowers.

III
MY FATHER'S TELESCOPE

Then I went an' stood up
On some high ol' lonesome hill
I went an' stood up
On some high ol' lonesome hill
An' looked down on the house
Where I used to live

—*Bessie Smith*

GRAPE SHERBET

The day? Memorial.
After the grill
Dad appears with his masterpiece—
swirled snow, gelled light.
We cheer. The recipe's
a secret and he fights
a smile, his cap turned up
so the bib resembles a duck.

That morning we galloped
through the grassed-over mounds
and named each stone
for a lost milk tooth. Each dollop
of sherbet, later,
is a miracle,
like salt on a melon that makes it sweeter.

Everyone agrees— it's wonderful!
It's just how we imagined lavender
would taste. The diabetic grandmother
stares from the porch,
a torch
of pure refusal.

We thought no one was lying
there under our feet,
we thought it
was a joke. I've been trying
to remember the taste,
but it doesn't exist.
Now I see why
you bothered,
father.

47

ROSES

It's time you learned something.
Halfway outdoors
he pauses, the flat dark fury of
his jaw, one eye, a shoulder in torn
blue cloth, the pruning shears
a mammoth claw resting
between meals.

                I scramble
up, terrified and down
the drive, the gravel's
brittle froth
and stand completely
helpless as he parts
a thousand pinkish eyelids
to find the beetles nested
at the root, teeming
disease.

They came from Japan, 1961.
They were nothing like the locusts
we hadn't noticed until they
were gone, the husks
sheer tuxedos
snagged on bark, the rafters,
the dying bayberry.

                It's easy—
pop them between your nails.
In the tool shed's populous

shadows, I hold the Mason jar instead
with both hands as he shakes
the flowers above
the kerosene which is shivering now
like the ocean I have never seen . . .

and I bear on a tray indoors
the inculpable, blushing prize.

SUNDAY NIGHT AT GRANDFATHER'S

He liked to joke and all of his jokes were practical.
The bent thumb jiggling between two ribs, his
Faked and drunken swoon. We tipped by and
He caught us, grandfather's right, right
Up to the cliff of his pure white
Shirt, real Fruit-of-the-
Loom. We shrieked and
He cackled like
A living
Ghost.

He hated Billy the parakeet, mean as half-baked sin.
He hated church-going women and the radio turned
Up loud. His favorite son, called Billy
Too, had flown the coop although
Each year he visited, each
Time from a different
City, gold
Tooth and
Drunk.

Then out came the cherry soda and potato chips and pretzel
Grandma humming hymns and rocking in the back bedroom
Dad holding Billy out on a thick and bitten finger,
Saying *Here: Come on Joe— touch him.*
Every Sunday night the same.
Dad's quiet urging and
That laugh: *You've*
Got to be
Kidding,
Son.

CENTIPEDE

With the storm moved on the next town
we take a flashlight down to the basement

Nested chairs stripped of varnish
Turpentine shadows stiff legs in the air

Look by the fusebox a centipede Dad says
I scream and let go of his hairy arm

MY FATHER'S TELESCOPE

The oldest joke
in the world,
a chair on three legs.

Sawdust kicks
up, swirls
around his boots

and settles
in the cuffs of his
pants. The saw is

as nervous as
a parrot.
The chair

shrinks. After
years of cupboards
and end tables, after

a plywood Santa
and seven elves
for the lawn in snow,

he knows.
He's failed, and
in oak.

Next Christmas
he buys himself
and his son

a telescope.

SONG. SUMMER

Sexless, my brother flies
over the house. He is glad
to have this dark vegetable
taken from him and hums

as he circles. The air
brims; already forgotten
his name and the beckoning
shapes below on the lawn.

In the evening my brother
dips, a dark cross fluttering.
He hears the eaves
murmur; he watches the open

mouth of my father. Now
he smiles, sailing
over the roof, heading
straight for the blue cloud

of pine.

ANTI-FATHER

Contrary to
tales you told us

summer nights when
the air conditioner

broke—the stars
are not far

apart. Rather
they draw

closer together
with years.

And houses
shrivel, un-lost,

and porches sag;
neighbors phone

to report cracks
in the cellar floor,

roots of the willow
coming up. Stars

speak to a child.
The past

is silent. . . .
Just between

me and you,
woman to man,

outer space is
inconceivably

intimate.

TO BED

We turn off
the light and
walk upstairs.
Scurrile moon
and a crazed
sniper hugging
the roof, a nickel
and its buffalo.
The house is
strange, the screen
padlocked
for luck, for
riches, for
love, the cup
of water in my
hands dark
as a well.
Dark swells. The
last one up
is the first
to go.

A FATHER OUT WALKING ON THE LAWN

Five rings light your approach across
the dark. You're lonely, anyone

can tell— so many of you
trembling, at the center the thick

dark root. Out here on a lawn
twenty-one years
gone under the haunches of a neighbor's

house, American Beauties
lining a driveway the mirror image of your own,

you wander, waiting to be
discovered. What
can I say to a body
that merely looks

like you? The willow, infatuated with its
surroundings, quakes; not that violent
orgasm nor the vain promise of

a rose relinquishing
its famous scent all for you, no,

not even the single
brilliant feather

a blue jay loses in flight
which dangles momentarily, azure scimitar,
above the warm eaves of your house—
nothing can change

this travesty, this
magician's skew of scarves
issuing from an opaque heart.

Who sees you anyway, except
at night, and with a fantastic eye?

If only you were bright enough to touch!

IV
PRIMER FOR THE NUCLEAR AGE

Doc, all my life people say
I was ugly. (pause) Makes me
feel mean.

—*Boris Karloff,*
    in The Raven

THE SAILOR IN AFRICA

a Viennese card game, circa 1910

There are two white captains
and two Moors. The pilots complement
their superiors, while the crew,
eight hands per master, wear
identical motley.
Available also, four ships
and a wild card
(starburst) which
luck can change into
a schooner or
a beautiful woman.

The captains, pilots, crews
commence
from the globe's four
corners. They share
a sun, a moon, and one
treasure. The goal
is Africa. One must uphold
the proportions between
superior and subordinate
while obtaining
chips. There are several cards
representing either
cannons or cannonballs
to make matters more
interesting. Plus a pair
of dice, for where
can we go without chance?

Say the Italian Moor
sails in sunshine
to Morocco and is rewarded
five black chips. Meanwhile
the British captain and
his swarthy pilot are stranded
with an overladen ship

somewhere between the Ibos and
Jamestown, Virginia.
The moon intrudes. When
the Spanish brigantine looms
on the horizon, they are actually
grateful, for they have cannons
and the Sevillian does not.

Both ships proceed
to Virginia. The arrow swings
east. Monsieur de la Roque
parades on deck, a small
white anchor stitched
on a blue field over
his heart. He surveys
his craft, finely strung
as a harp. *If all goes well
we'll reach Santo Domingo
tomorrow.* . . .

By now the Italian vessel
is safely through
the Suez Canal,
but a card shows "gale"
and it runs aground
on the western shore
of Madagascar, miraculously
unscathed. The captain falls
asleep on the beach, dreaming
of gold. Awake, he finds
ship and crew vanished, the
sun grinning and the treasure
secure at the bottom of the deck.
—Will he,

like the Spanish Moor,
be sold, merchant
to merchandise, or will
wild boars discover
him first? Monsieur de la Roque
has landed at Santo Domingo,
picking up a rum and a slave
named Pedro. Such
flashing eyes and refined
manners! He'll make
an excellent valet.

Adrift in the Atlantic
again, the Englishman
plays quoits with his pilot,
his eyes raw
from staring into the sun.
A desperate man, he will
choose the beautiful woman
and die.

While Pedro— who,
it turns out, is none other
than the Captain from Seville,
has loosened the leg irons
and drugged the fastidious
de la Roque! Now the
white anchor heaves
on the breast of the Moor, and
the sun beams on the mutinous

crew of his brother, who have
cleared the Cape of
Good Hope and are bearing

down on the Guinea coast.
Pedro heads

for Brazil— the women there,
he's heard, are prodigious!
Then the arrow swerves
due south, "gale" shows
from nowhere, the treasure
drops to the ocean floor.
At the sight of so many
mountains surging
whitely ahead, a crew hand,
thinking he has gone
to hell, falls
overboard, his red sash
flaring. Even

Pedro, lashed to the mast,
believes he has glimpsed
through the storm's
pearly membrane
God's dark face swooping
down to kiss— as the main
sail, incandescent under
pressure, bursts
like a star. The ship
splinters
on the rocks

                    just as, deep
in the Madagascan forests,
a black hand
lifts from a nest

an egg the bright
green of malachite. . . .

At least one man happy
to have lost everything.
His crew will make it home
with tales of strange lands
and their captain's untimely
demise.

In the Atlantic,
windstill.
The English vessel, so
close to home, stalls.
Nothing for them to do
but pass the time
playing cards.

EARLY MORNING
ON THE TEL AVIV—HAIFA FREEWAY

The shore is cabbage green and reeks.
Reclaimed swamp sprouts citrus
and tamarisk, manna to the ancients
who were starved for miracles.
Now a paper mill and Alliance Tires
spill their secrets further out to sea.

Along the roadside, two Arab boys
drag a gull by the wings
and beyond a horse belly-up in the field.
A glider dips over us, silent, and
gleams as it turns. We should stop
but drive on.

WHY I TURNED VEGETARIAN

Mister Minister, I found
the tip of your thumb
bit off a way back:
a neat cap. Begging
your pardon, perhaps
you'd miss it
sooner or later.
You probably dropped it
folding the newspaper.

I don't mean to intrude.
I saw no other way less painful
or designed. It was lying
where I couldn't fail
to spot it— still fresh
with color and ridges
and a sliver of nail
and the teeth marks
showing— the only
edible mushroom
in the whole plot of grass.

EASTERN EUROPEAN ECLOGUES

I

This melodious
prison: crowds
shivering around
the sausage stalls.

II

One of us will
suffer. Don't move.
Not one word
more. You're
imagining things.

III

All that's quiet
is magic. Fields
steaming with dung.
Fresh meat in the air.

IV

One of us will need
a month in the country
to ward off imminent
complications.

V

Who?
Of course not.
Why should they.
Of course not.

VI

The countryside
is lovely
this time of year

FLIRTATION

After all, there's no need
to say anything

at first. An orange, peeled
and quartered, flares

like a tulip on a wedgwood plate.
Anything can happen. `

Outside the sun
has rolled up her rugs

and night strewn salt
across the sky. My heart

is humming a tune
I haven't heard in years!

Quiet's cool flesh—
let's sniff and eat it.

There are ways
to make of the moment

a topiary
so the pleasure's in

walking through.

EXEUNT THE VIOLS

with their throb and yearn, their sad
stomach of an alley cat. Listen:

even the ocean mourns the passage
of voices so pure and penetrant, that

insect hum. Who discovered usefulness?
Who forgot how to sing, simply?

(Magnificence spoke up briefly, followed
by the race boat's break-neck

dazzle.) A tremor rises in the throat
of the cat, the quill jerks in the hand

of the melancholy scribe. The gambas
beat a retreat, gracefully—

their last chord a breath drawn
deep in a garden maze, there

near the statue
smiling under the stars.

THE LEFT—HANDED CELLIST

You came with a cello in one hand,
in the other, nothing.
Play, you said.

I played the scales of ignorant evenings.
I played in high heels to be closer to you.

When you snapped off a stem
from the vase, you broke
my little finger.

This is a theme in mauve:
it begins with the children's blind bodies,
it ends with the boys in the orchestra.

Tell me that you did not profit from me,
you with the pewter hands.

LINES MUTTERED IN SLEEP

Black chest hairs, soft sudden mass.
Washed up on her breast his pale and startled face.
Pine scent, lake scent, gorse scent, bark.

PRIMER FOR THE NUCLEAR AGE

At the edge of the mariner's
    map is written: "Beyond
    this point lie Monsters."

Someone left the light on
    in the pantry—there's
    a skull in there on the shelf

that talks. Blue eyes
    in the air, blue as
    an idiot's. Any fear, any

memory will do; and if you've
    got a heart at all, someday
    it will kill you.

PARSLEY

1. *The Cane Fields*

There is a parrot imitating spring
in the palace, its feathers parsley green.
Out of the swamp the cane appears

to haunt us, and we cut it down. El General
searches for a word; he is all the world
there is. Like a parrot imitating spring,

we lie down screaming as rain punches through
and we come up green. We cannot speak an R—
out of the swamp, the cane appears

and then the mountain we call in whispers *Katalina.*
The children gnaw their teeth to arrowheads.
There is a parrot imitating spring.

El General has found his word: *perejil.*
Who says it, lives. He laughs, teeth shining
out of the swamp. The cane appears

in our dreams, lashed by wind and streaming.
And we lie down. For every drop of blood
there is a parrot imitating spring.
Out of the swamp the cane appears.

2. *The Palace*

The word the general's chosen is parsley.
It is fall, when thoughts turn
to love and death; the general thinks
of his mother, how she died in the fall
and he planted her walking cane at the grave
and it flowered, each spring stolidly forming
four-star blossoms. The general

pulls on his boots, he stomps to
her room in the palace, the one without
curtains, the one with a parrot
in a brass ring. As he paces he wonders
Who can I kill today. And for a moment
the little knot of screams
is still. The parrot, who has traveled

all the way from Australia in an ivory
cage, is, coy as a widow, practising
spring. Ever since the morning
his mother collapsed in the kitchen
while baking skull-shaped candies
for the Day of the Dead, the general
has hated sweets. He orders pastries
brought up for the bird; they arrive

dusted with sugar on a bed of lace.
The knot in his throat starts to twitch;
he sees his boots the first day in battle
splashed with mud and urine
as a soldier falls at his feet amazed—
how stupid he looked!— at the sound
of artillery. *I never thought it would sing*
the soldier said, and died. Now

the general sees the fields of sugar
cane, lashed by rain and streaming.
He sees his mother's smile, the teeth
gnawed to arrowheads. He hears
the Haitians sing without R's
as they swing the great machetes:
Katalina, they sing, *Katalina*,

mi madle, mi amol en muelte. God knows
his mother was no stupid woman; she
could roll an R like a queen. Even
a parrot can roll an R! In the bare room
the bright feathers arch in a parody
of greenery, as the last pale crumbs
disappear under the blackened tongue. Someone

76

calls out his name in a voice
so like his mother's, a startled tear
splashes the tip of his right boot.
My mother, my love in death.
The general remembers the tiny green sprigs
men of his village wore in their capes
to honor the birth of a son. He will
order many, this time, to be killed

for a single, beautiful word.

NOTES

Tou Wan Speaks to Her Husband, Liu Sheng: Liu Sheng, Prince Ching of Chung Shan, died in 113 B.C. He and his wife lived in the middle of the Western Han Dynasty. Their tombs were unearthed west of Mancheng, Hopei Province, in 1968.

Catherine of Alexandria: (died 307?). She rebuked the Roman emperor Galerius Valerius Maximinus, who then condemned her to be broken on the wheel. The wheel miraculously disintegrated.

Catherine of Siena: (1347-1380). A wool merchant's daughter, Catherine refused to marry. She received the stigmata and worked to secure peace between the Papacy and a divided Italy, dictating letters of advice to people all over Europe.

Shakespeare Say: Champion Jack Dupree, black American blues singer, is now living and touring in Europe.

Banneker: Benjamin Banneker (1731-1806), first black man to devise an almanac and predict a solar eclipse accurately, was also appointed to the commission that surveyed and laid out what is now Washington, D.C.

Agosta the Winged Man and Rasha the Black Dove: Christian Schad (1894-1982) painted the two sideshow entertainers in Berlin in 1929. (see book cover)

Parsley: On October 2, 1957, Rafael Trujillo (1891-1961), dictator of the Dominican Republic, ordered 20,000 blacks killed because they could not pronounce the letter "r" in *perejil*, the Spanish word for parsley.

Carnegie M

Bell, *Stars Which See, Stars Which Do Not See*

Dobyns, *Black Dog, Red Dog*

ve, *Museum*

ve, *The Yel   on the Corner*

D   , *Full of Lust and G od Usage*

Fo , *The Town Clock Burning*

Inez, *The Woman Who Loved Worms
                              and Other Poems*

      evis, *The Dollmaker's Ghost*

Thomas Lux, *Sunday*

Jack Matthews, *An Almanac for Twilight*

Dave Smith, *The Fisherman's Whore*

Maura Stanton, *Cries of Swimmers*

Gerald Stern, *Two Long Poems*

James Tate, *Absences*